Collect the Cash

The Sale is Not Complete Until the Money is in the Bank!

Dee Bowden

Foreword By: Dr. Cassandra Bradford

Publishing Service By: Pen Legacy®
Editing & Typesetting By: Carla M. Dean, U Can Mark My Word
Cover By: Junnita Jackson

Library of Congress Cataloging – in-Publication Data has been applied for.

Paperback ISBN: 978-1-7364112-7-8
Electronic Book ISBN: 978-1-7364112-6-1

PRINTED IN THE UNITED STATES OF AMERICA

Table of Contents

Foreword

To know Dee is to become absolutely amazed at her knowledge about money, cash, collections, and all things concerning "getting your money back." My first meeting with Dee in Los Angeles, California, reminds me of the passionate conversation we had about her endeavors and the beautiful vision that God has placed inside her involving her business journey.

Since that time, I have seen Dee explode! It appears she ran out of the gate with both feet moving, arms pumping, and eyes fixed on the prize—full speed ahead and without warning. I've watched the adrenaline she's displayed, and it makes me, and any other entrepreneur, stop and wonder whether we are moving fast enough, forward enough, and brave enough. Dee's example is a clear indication that she is a child after God's own heart, meaning taking the directive seriously, running the course, pursuing the passion, and igniting the world with her talents, gifts, and abilities. Now, she has enabled her footprint by writing this book, *Collect the Cash*, which is a testament that God does what He says he will do.

If this book doesn't open your eyes about money, cash, and the pursuit thereof, then close the book and read it again.

Thank you, Dee, for sharing your expertise with me and the world!

Cassandra

Dr. Cassandra Bradford
International, Award-Winning Consultant,
Certification Expert, and Mentor
Genesis Preferred Solutions

What People Are Saying About
Collect the Cash

It is the goal of every business to turn a profit. You create a product or services. You get customers. You get paid. Sounds simple enough, right? But anyone in business long enough will tell you it's not always that easy. Clients don't pay. Invoices pile up. Money's not coming in, and you've still got a business to run. Now what?

Get your hands on this book! In her new release, Collect the Cash, Dee Bowden, financial strategist, and master of her craft, debunks the scary myths about collections and provides a deep dive into why businesses don't get paid. With over 10 years and $13 million in outstanding debt collected, Dee breaks down the principal stages of a sales cycle and teaches business owners how to secure their cash flow.

She provides practical examples on how to identify and correct the breakdowns in your money-making process and increase your bottom line. Collect the Cash is empowering, inspiring, and immediately helpful. Dee's mantra "The sale is not complete until the money is in the bank" is an absolute testament to why this book is a must-read for anyone doing business today.

Sharai Robbin, Simon & Schuster Bestselling Author
CEO, Good Ground Literary Services

Dee Bowden

It is said that "experience is a good teacher" and when it comes to the niche world of collections, Dee Bowden has a wealth of lived experience on all sides of the issue. As an artist and entrepreneur, I have parts of my business life that I enjoy thoroughly, which are things I'm comfortable with, but other parts like "collecting the cash" aren't as comfortable. But alas, as we all know, business isn't business without money. It's vital to make deals for your goods or services, but the deal isn't real until the money is in the bank! Dee can walk you the rest of the way to having your Accounts Receivable become Accounts Receivable Received!

Eva Jane Bunkley
Eva Jane Beauty, LLC - Inventor of "The Makeup Bullet®"

The warmth, humor, and honesty that you will find in these pages will help any entrepreneur with cashflow problems due to uncollected AR. Dee is able to take an often intimidating and unpleasant task and break down the process into easily manageable steps that will provide the courage and understanding to not only do well, but EXCEL! This is a definite MUST-READ!

Renée Myers
Owner/Cake Artist, The Golden Rose Cakery

Dee is a money saver, literally. She saves you from potentially lost revenue and more money spent trying to recover it. She also saves you time and energy that could be used focusing on the health of your business. Collect the Cash is the obvious next step in educating business owners about the importance of having a positive cash flow with fewer losses due to the negative effects of unpaid invoices.

Cheryl Polote-Williamson
Global Media Executive, Award-Winning, Best-Selling
Author and Speaker

Introduction

Congratulations! I'm so glad you've made a conscious decision to ensure your business is financially secure by not leaving money on the table. So often in business, companies fail not because they don't have sales but merely due to a lack of operating cash. This can happen simply because their practices and systems for getting paid were not sufficient, thus doing business "for free." With my experience and knowledge within this arena, it is my duty to help prepare business owners to win...and win big! It is my hope that once you finish this book, you will be an expert on collecting the cash and having longevity in business.

You may be wondering how I am qualified to speak on this topic of collecting cash. Well, let me share my story...

While working as a part-time collections clerk for an IT company, I was given a list of accounts with past due invoices (30/60/90 days) that totaled $8 million. It was my job to get all accounts paid in full. I was super excited for the challenge but immediately went into prayer, asking for wisdom on how to recover this money. After my spirit and faith were calm, I went to work and collected $6 million in 60 days. Then, the unthinkable occurred!

One day, the CEO said, "I want to thank everybody for your time. I appreciate all your services, but we have made an executive decision. We are closing the company. You have thirty minutes to go get your stuff and leave the building." Can you say unexpected? After all the work, time, and energy I had invested in collecting and getting the company paid, I was let go along with about 100 people. While collecting that much money was impressive, losing my job made me take a closer look at businesses and how money drives them.

Even though the company had a team of collectors and I alone had collected $6 million dollars, it was not enough to keep the doors open. It's obvious more things came into play than us just recovering the money, but the bottom line was, there was more money on the books than in the bank. It was in that moment I came up with the quote, *"The sale is not complete until the money is in the bank."* From that experience, I realized some companies become so focused on the product, the sale, and the next contract that they neglect the back-end office. That is what happened with the company I worked for and possibly to many of you. You may have a business or various income streams but not enough income to sustain your doors remaining open.

Since this experience, my career has been in receivables management, collections, and contract administration post-award. Basically, once a contract is awarded, I have dealt with the vendors to ensure they have received payment for services rendered, regardless if it's a private sector company or a government agency. Thus, my career path led me to birth my business, BCS Solutions—a revenue recovery company that helps businesses untangle the money disconnects and recover lost revenue, lost time, and mitigate business decline. I am on a mission to help entrepreneurs, small businesses, and corporations grow their financial bottom line by instituting reputable systems that will invoice and ensure that cash is received on payday. The methods I use work, and to date, I have recovered millions of dollars and counting! I have been featured in *Forbes*, *Black Enterprise* and *Thrive Global* magazines and have shared the stage at the Success Women's Conference with Lisa Nichols, Iyanla Vanzant, Robin Roberts (GMA), Gloria Mayfield Banks (Mary Kay Cosmetics), and others.

In this book, *Collect the Cash: The Sale is Not Complete Until the Money is in the Bank*, I offer my successful strategies for collecting payments. I will also share some proven processes on how to become confident in collections, along with tips and approaches that will empower and remind you that being in business requires an operating cash flow that will sustain you. As Warren Buffet said, *"Rule No.1: Never lose money. Rule No.2: Never forget rule No.1."*

Are you ready to win? Let's get started.

Mindset Over Money

As a business owner, collections require a mindset not to leave money on the table. I believe building strong relationships across departments is necessary. I discovered this process throughout my career. I worked for companies with several departments that collectively impacted my ability to collect **old** and **owed** invoices. To collect the outstanding invoices, I first had to identify the problem and mentally prepare to solve it.

Most people who perform collections/accounts receivables discover early in their career that they are good problem solvers, researchers, and detail oriented. That was me. I always wanted to know *the why* behind *the what* when it came to collecting outstanding invoices. Being inquisitive, I would ask the question, "How long has this invoice been sitting here not paid?" I initially see collections as two things: problem-solving and an extension of customer service.

I never knew much about mindset. How you think can have

an impact on everything around you. This truth became more evident when I was assigned an $8-million-dollar accounts receivable problem with no real plan to solve it at the time. Based on the number of issues I had resolved previously; I knew I was a smart problem solver. By closing out government contracts, I collected millions of dollars and realized my thought process and the steps I took to resolve it led to a mindset over money.

One scripture I recited every day was Matthew 18:18 (Amplified). Jesus said, "Whatever you loose on earth shall have been loosed in heaven." Therefore, I "loosed" the finances owed to this company. I called money to come in, so these accounts were paid in Jesus' name! I learned this statement and principle in a book by Charles Capps called *God's Creative Power for Finances.* In reviewing the section on collecting money and accounts receivables, I knew I struck gold. I decided to take my accounts receivable aging reports and start declaring this confession every day. I worked to get my daily mindset ready to address these issues.

Once I started down the road of daily affirmations and doing the work to collect the money, I started seeing some success. Adding affirmations to my daily routine became a game-changer for me. See, when I first went to work for the company, I was very new to affirmations and speaking positive words out loud. It seemed quite silly to think that making declarations out loud over past due accounts would make a difference. Then I learned something that other business owners may be able to relate to and might find beneficial.

It wasn't enough to make the declarations; I still had to make the calls, address any challenges, and work with customers to resolve issues. Years later, I would discover how important it was to have the right mindset for collections when a former employer told me that I knew nothing about collections or contract closeouts (collections for government agencies) and fired me. Yes, I got fired because he listened to the comments of someone who never closed out a government contract nor knew the steps needed to make sure everything was completed. After being fired, I leaned on my faith and new affirmations. I landed a job with the second-largest transportation company in the US, where I successfully audited contracts and won Contract File Auditor four times for achievement. I learned to take my rejection and use it as motivational fuel to bounce back from a devastating blow. My faith, hard work, and determination helped me overcome the negative perceptions of collections/accounts receivable and not give up on pursuing my dreams and being successful in my career. I went on to work at a large government agency and successfully recovered $7.5 million dollars in one year. Every success I have achieved after that painful day was because I got into the collections zone, refocused my attention and energy, and added my faith to everything I do. Has it been smooth sailing? Absolutely not. Nothing worth having or achieving comes without hard work, growth, and being open to pivoting, as necessary.

The Importance of Knowing How to Collect Money

What I have figured out in this business is some companies have a collections team, but often, the team is told, "Meet the quota. Get the numbers. Get the money." No one ever sits down with them and asks, "Okay, do you have a strategy for how you are going to collect the outstanding balance?"

I attribute my success in collections to many things, but it would be an uphill battle without these four key factors: **Problem-solving, Excellent Customer Service, Relationship Management,** and **Gratitude**. You must give them an equal weight of importance to see a change with your revenue recovery process.

Case in point. One of my former employers was a value-added reseller. They had a team of collectors and amassed $45 million worth of sales. They dealt in different sectors, one of which was with the federal government. One of the collectors on the team did not know how to collect from the federal government. He didn't know any of the acronyms, nor did he understand government contracting. Management told him, "Here's your list of accounts; go to work." I saw this as a problem.

As a business owner, if you are not taking the time to teach your employees how to collect from business to government, business to business, and business to corporate, then you're not going to collect your money. Collections is not just dialing for dollars. You must know your industry, the proper terminology, and the way those industry-specific systems work. To help him out, we held a Collections roundtable. It was my way of saying, "Come sit with me, and bring your accounts. Let's go over what you don't understand and let me teach you how to do this more effectively." I shared the knowledge with the other collections team members, five in total, who all learned how to collect successfully. I am happy to say that in 90 days, because of doing the roundtable, we collected $33 million, and the company has been on track ever since.

From there, I started teaching the collectors because **THEY** are the people on the front lines, not the Chief Executive Officer (CEO) or the Chief Financial Officer (CFO)! I think some businesses forget it's the worker bee that gets the work done. They are sometimes taken for granted and not recognized for their hard work to collect the cash. The CEO and CFO are not usually making the calls. The people doing the day-to-day work are the ones who need to be taught how to do this. If you do not know how to think analytically or resolve a problem, you are not likely to recover your money. Focus on solving the problem!

Your business is not solely about the sale, getting the contract signed, or delivering the product. If you have not gotten paid after 30, 60, or even 90 days, something is amiss with your collections process. That means you must go back and research. In each step along the way, you must ask yourself crucial questions, going back to the beginning of the paper trail:

- Did the company meet and address the terms?
- Did you deliver the product?
- Did you prepare and submit a proper invoice?

One must also consider how many hands (departments) are involved in collections, such as sales, contracts, and accounting. In this company's case, the amount of uncollected money left on the books was due to these departments not interacting. Many businesses make the mistake of operating these areas independently of each other instead of properly integrating them into the complete sales cycle. The issue is that most business owners do not even understand what a complete sales cycle is or how it works. Not knowing this or having it in place, along with not following up to make sure all the steps in the sales process happens, results in business owners leaving uncollected money on the table.

To debunk your ideas about money and collections, I need you to see money for what it is—a necessary tool and resource for your business. While you should focus on the next proposal or quote and get the sale, you still need to collect the payments owed for sales already made. Your services and products are worth being paid for, and what you provide in the marketplace matters! Do not devalue yourself or your business by not collecting on your invoices. Let's keep it real! Leaving cash on the table could mean there will be people and bills that go unpaid because there is not enough money to do so, which may lead to downsizing and layoffs. As a business owner, you never want to get to that point.

Understand Cash Flow

Before we get into the strategies for collecting the cash, let us better understanding how cash flow relates to your business.

Cash flow is like a puzzle. It has five key pieces, which we will explore shortly: Sales, Contracts, Orders, Invoices, and Payments. In simpler terms, cash flow is the money that should be moving (flowing) in and out of your business monthly. Although it sometimes seems cash flows only one way (out of the business), it needs to flow both ways for the company to stay afloat. Examples of cash going out of your business would be expenses for rent or a mortgage, utilities, payroll, loan payments, and payments for taxes and other accounts payable.

Cash comes in from customers or clients who purchase products or services. If customers don't pay when making their purchase or after receiving a service, the cash flow may come from account receivable collections or past due invoices. There are four buckets for accounts receivable related to the invoice terms:

- ➢ 0-30-day invoices
- ➢ 31-60-day invoices
- ➢ 61-90-day invoices
- ➢ 91-plus-day invoices

If you are not paid based on the invoice terms set with the client or customer, it creates an outstanding debt on your books. In turn, this could create a negative effect on your cash flow, especially if your business is operating on a cash basis. Therefore, you need invoices paid timely to run your business.

If customers aren't paying, it doesn't always mean they are all deadbeats or debt-dodgers. The problem could likely have started with your business process—the cash flow process.

Earlier, I alluded to the cash flow process having five puzzle pieces. These five puzzle pieces are **interconnected**, and without one of these pieces working correctly, it can cause a breakdown in the collections process and have you chasing your money. This visual should help you better understand how everything fits together:

Are you feeling like a deer in headlights? Well, let me simplify it a little more by using the example of purchasing a cell phone—not the kind where you add minutes, but the one where you have a contract.

Since cell phones can be quite expensive, major carriers offer a payment plan through a signed contract. They get you to agree to patronize them through excellent customer service and showing gratitude for giving them the sale. Once you enter into a signed agreement, you have essentially bought goods (phone) and service (data plan/minutes). Once you leave the store, you have agreed to pay the invoice, with terms that are generally net 30 days. Your payments help keep the company in business and your phone service active. Non-payment has consequences for both parties. They can report you to the credit bureau, thus ruining your credit, and your service will be disconnected if the bill remains unpaid, leading to dissatisfaction on both sides. *Can you hear me now, business owners?*

I hope this now provides more clarity on the cash flow process. A slow or negative cash flow will keep you up at night! Like most business owners, you worry about Days Sales Outstanding (DSO) — a measure of how long it takes your business to convert receivables into cash. The goal is to have the sale complete and the money in the bank. For every sales transaction that takes place, there is a process that identifies when your business will receive approximate payments.

So, by not collecting your owed money, you are putting your business at risk, something I do not want for your company. As a business owner, you have already invested time, energy, and capital. While managing your cash flow and tracking the state of your accounts, you should always have the mindset that losing money is not an option and that revenue recovery is necessary to stay solvent. This is important because you will be planning for and forecasting your growth!

If you see cash flow issues, I encourage you to talk to your managers and take some time to investigate why there is a bottleneck with getting paid in a timely manner.

Case Study I: Where is the Money?

Hopefully, you now understand how important it is to collect the cash and have a positive cash flow. But we have only reached the tip of the iceberg regarding the collections process. Allow me to share an example of how one company struggled to collect a substantial outstanding debt, which I resolved with ONE phone call.

Remember how I mentioned that working in collections involves problem-solving and an extension of customer service? Well, I had an account that owed our company $2 million. The account was 60 to 90 days past due, which meant I needed to investigate. So, I placed a call and asked to speak with the Accounts Payable department. After exchanging pleasantries, I asked why the invoices had not been paid. The Accounts Payable manager explained that the company changed over to a new billing system and that until we submitted the invoices in the required new format, we wouldn't get paid. Since I had no knowledge of this change within their company, it was certainly news to me. After requesting a copy of the email announcing the change, I thanked them for taking my call and explaining the delay in paying the past-due amount. Then I stated that I would get the revised invoices submitted ASAP. Once I received the email, I shared it with the comptroller, who was in disbelief. For the next week, I focused on nothing else but working on getting those invoices reformatted to that company's new billing system and resubmitted for payment. I'm happy to report the client paid the invoices.

Following up and being persistent is key when it comes to sealing the deal. As you see, customer service has a lot to do with collections. If your customers aren't happy with the products or services (*or, in this case, if the invoices are not in the right format)*, they may choose to withhold payments…and you certainly don't want a delay in receiving the money that is due to you.

Encouragement for New Entrepreneurs

If you are a new business owner, no doubt you are in business to make money. While it is thrilling to run your own business, whether full-time or part-time, you'll still need to have safeguards in place to ensure your business is financially successful, which means having a positive cash flow. The experiences I shared talked about recovering millions of dollars, but it doesn't matter if you are owed ten million or ten dollars. If you delivered everything per your contractual obligations, you should be paid in full and on time. When money does not come in as planned, it will have a negative effect on the way you do business.

Debt recovery is not for the weak of heart. Many people find asking for money uncomfortable, even nerve-wracking, but you need to remember that your business can only function with paying customers or clients. Your motivation to make money is the reason you decided to embark on entrepreneurship. Unless you are a philanthropist, you didn't start your business to give away free products and services. So, if you open that "free" door, be prepared for people to run through it and run over you. While most customers intend to pay, some will take your kindness for weakness and try not to honor the agreement, which is the exchange of goods or services for monetary payment. Go after what you are owed without hesitation, remorse, or guilt. It doesn't matter the amount because an unpaid invoice for ten dollars can quickly turn into unpaid thousands.

As a start-up business, you should always receive payment. "Free" should not be an acceptable term. If you want to show your customers appreciation for their loyalty and support, there are better ways to do this than giving away your products or services, such as offering bonuses and perks. As a matter of fact, I strongly encourage you to reward customers who make timely payments; it's a great way to retain your customer base. You can reward them by offering rebates, coupons, discounts, loyalty points, etc.

No matter if you are a company of 1 or 100, you still need processes or systems in place to manage cash flow and keep track of your invoices. Finance and accounting don't come easy to everybody, but don't fret. There are several software packages you can choose from to purchase to help manage invoices, such as the extremely popular QuickBooks. Please do your research to find the software that will be best for your business.

While you are deciding on the type of accounting software you might need, you may want to start using Microsoft Excel. In Excel, you can easily create columns and input the information for your customer or client accounts. This will provide you with a quick snapshot of your company's financial status. Helpful columns to include are:

1. Customers' contact information
2. Date of invoices sent
3. Date of payments received
4. Calculations showing monies owed or a zeroed-out balance

Using formulas in Excel, which can do automatic calculations, will save you a lot of time. This can be your Basic Tracking Sheet. Later, I will explain how to use a tracker, especially in the area of debt recovery.

If you are not familiar with Excel, consider attending YouTube University. It's not an actual college, but there is a wealth of free online knowledge and "how-to" videos on using Excel and other software programs. Additionally, your local community college and Small Business Administration may offer classes and courses to help you manage your finances.

Lastly, depending on your budget, consider hiring a virtual assistant or other administrative help with a background in accounting and/or bookkeeping. Companies, such as the one I founded, can handle all these processes on your behalf. As your business grows, you will probably need to have designated staff or departments to assist with your paperwork, such as accounts payable and accounts receivable departments. I will discuss this in subsequent chapters, as well. The thing to remember is you don't have to do this alone. Whichever way you choose to go, please do not delay initiating a method to keep track of your sales, invoices, and payments so you can be successful financially. I'm rooting for you!

Build a Strong Collections Team

Let's talk a little bit about your staff. I've shared that your mindset is important when doing this type of work. The right attitude plays an essential part in how successful you are with revenue recovery. People who do this for a living have to *love* it. They must be detail and goal-oriented, patient, and not mind doing the research.

As a business owner, you should consider having the following collections team or departments in place depending on your company's size. In small businesses or as a solo-prenuer, this could be one or two people, but in larger organizations, these roles would be strategically placed throughout the organization:

- **Sales:** Person or team of people dedicated to closing the deal; ensure products, goods, or services are sold.
- **Contracts**: Person or team of people who ensure signed

contracts and agreements are in good order with explicit terms.

- **Accounts Payable**: Person or team of people who execute outgoing payments.
- **Accounts Receivables**: Person or team of people responsible for receiving incoming payments and applying them to existing invoices.

I urge you to establish a solid collaboration between Accounts Receivables and Sales. Get the Sales and Accounts Receivable departments to see the value of having a good working relationship with each other along with the other vital departments to foster successful business operations.

Case Study II: Where is the Money?

When I worked for a tech company, they had a collections team of five people. The Chief Financial Officer was extremely frustrated that over $40 million dollars was outstanding, and the team couldn't handle it. So, right out the gate, it was implied the team was ill-equipped. They were a tough crowd. No one really cared for or engaged with them as people; the focus was on meeting the quotas.

This was an indication that there were internal and external problems that had to be addressed. Staff morale plays a big part in ensuring a successful outcome, no matter the assigned task. Giving your staff recognition and providing ongoing training lets your staff know you have confidence in their skills and believe in their ability to get the job done. Creating a dynamic team means putting the team first. If you are the manager, consider leading by example. Roll up your sleeves and work alongside to see the intricacies of the process while, at the same time, learning the business from the inside out.

I was hired as a Collections Manager to get owed invoices collected by figuring out the disconnects and to get the team excited and motivated about collections again. While getting to know the team, I came across one team member assigned collections for government agencies. After we spoke, it was revealed that he didn't understand how to effectively collect from the government and therefore didn't like collections. Even though the team received training, it wasn't enough. After we did some one-on-one instruction and training sessions, she shared these remarks:

"Dee and I have been working together more closely on my accounts. Her assistance and being available to work directly with me helped me improve my 31 to 60 days past due accounts from $1.2 million to under $500K in days because she implemented the daily quick reviews. I wanted to let you know that progress has been made in a matter of days. Mentoring and teamwork definitely make a difference."

Taking responsibility for the success of the team wasn't easy, but it was necessary. When we met the goals and reduced the outstanding invoices, it raised self-esteem and confidence, which positively affected all involved. Please keep in mind your staff reflects you, your company, and your brand. Not only is

Dee Bowden

gratitude a useful tool for retaining customers, saying "Thank You" to your colleagues goes a long way.

Tips for Successful Collections

Now I'm going to let you into my vault of tools and tips for collecting the cash. As with anything, nothing is 100% foolproof. I'm going to be optimistic that you've done your due diligence with your clientele, and these tips should complement your business's processes.

Tip #1: Reminders & Nudges

How good does it feel when after a long day, you get that text message or voicemail that says, *Tomorrow is your appointment at 9 a.m.* We lead such busy lives that it is easy to forget appointments, meetings, gatherings, even parties. It can be the same way for the customer.

When setting up reminders, remember it's an effective communications strategy and good customer service. Rather than a demand for payment, these periodic nudges serve to keep customers in good standing so you can continue providing products and services.

Clear and open communication between your company and your customer is the key to successfully managing collections and accounts receivable. Prevent uncomfortable misunderstandings by staying in contact throughout the billing cycle. You'll enjoy a better relationship with the people buying from you, resulting in more sales and continued growth.

Most clients want to pay for their invoices, but life often gets in the way of even the most organized person. If you want to ensure that you receive your payments on time, reminders are good customer service but a tedious, high-maintenance function. However, the rewards can be worth all the time and energy spent to make sure your money is in the bank.

To attempt to avoid the collection call that no one wants to make or quite frankly receive, set up a process to remind customers about invoices at various times during the billing cycle. There are several times to send out these messages:

- Call within a week after payment is due to find out what is delaying the payment and strive to get a payment commitment from the customer. For delinquent accounts, while speaking with the customer, you can politely remind them of their prior promise to pay. For example, "When we spoke on Tuesday, June 20th, you promised payment by June 15th."
- Contact them before the due date to alert customers of upcoming payments.

- Reach out to them on the due date to ensure on-time payment.
- Call after the due date to prevent excessive accruing of late fees.

It is not a good practice to wait until an invoice is overdue. Sending out reminders to customers who owe money will tilt the wheel in your favor, and they will be much happier to hear from your company before their account becomes delinquent. Busy customers who might otherwise miss payment deadlines remain in good standing, so you don't have to worry about handling an awkward collections conversation.

Here's another way to save time. If you must speak with them on the phone, while you are still on the phone with them, send out the replacement invoices. Ask the customer to confirm they received the email and verify the payment method agreed upon during the call.

Does following this prescription of reminders to the letter mean you'll never have to make a collection call? Unfortunately, no. Invoices get lost, unexpected circumstances delay payment, and customers forget their due dates. When making collection calls, keep in mind that the point isn't to force a customer to pay. You are calling to resolve a potential problem, possibly something over which they had no control.

Tip #2: Make It Easy for the Customer to Pay You

This may seem like common sense, but it is an element that is often overlooked. In this fast-paced virtual world, people want to receive their money as fast as possible. Popular methods for the fast exchange of cash are:

- ACH (Automatic Clearing House): This is a transfer system that connects all the financial institutions, banks, and credit unions in the US.
- EFT (Electronic Funds Transfer): This is a way to move money between accounts at different banks electronically and works with the ACH. For example, if you are paid via direct deposit, that's a form of ACH and EFT transfer working together.
- Wire Transfer: This is a **transfer** of **funds** done electronically across a network of **banks** or **transfer** agencies worldwide. This method usually involves a fee. If you've ever used Western Union, it is like a wire transfer.

Checks and money orders are other forms of payment. The most used delivery method would be the United States Postal Service (USPS). Although USPS is often affectionately referred to as "snail mail", it's still a viable option. Some may also choose to use FedEx or UPS. For those who are leery of mobile banking and cash transfer apps, they will appreciate having these options to submit their payments.

The other payment processes your company could offer would be setting up automatic debits. That way, you aren't waiting for the customer to send in the money. It may require some administrative setup on the front end, but it almost guarantees you'll get paid on time.

Either way, to be competitive, offer all standard payment options. The more options you offer, the fewer chances you'll encounter someone making excuses for why they can't make the payment on time.

Here are some other ways you can ensure you'll receive timely payments:

- Make sure your outgoing invoices have the correct contact and contract information.
- Include a phone number, email, or other contact information for billing inquiries at your company.
- Use invoices that make it easy for the customer to remit and easy for them to keep a record of the invoice and payment.
- Confirm the customer is aware of the different methods.

Tip #3: Create a Collections Process

You may be wondering, *Why do I need to set up a collections process?* If you think about it, everything has a system or way that things are done. For your business, you should have documented guidance or a business process for anyone to follow. This will also keep things consistent.

Without procedures in place, this could lead to gaps and holes in your operational process. Additionally, once you experience exponential growth, your books should go through a regular audit process to ensure every "I" is dotted, and every "T" is crossed. The audit process will also identify any mistakes or inconsistencies with your collections process, which is important. Regular reviews help safeguard your business against detrimental mistakes and reduce costly errors if the process is done regularly with your staff.

But what is a collections *process*, you might ask? Is it more than just picking up the phone and asking for your money? Yes. There are certain "tools of the trade" you should utilize to help with collecting unpaid money.

Keep in mind that there are different processes depending on your type of business. Most of my experience is business-to-government; however, these tools should help you, even if you are business-to-business or business-to-consumer.

When you start analyzing your books and noticing there is outstanding money owed, you want to run an **aging report**. With this report, I suggest you start with what is commonly called "low hanging fruit" and deal with those first. If you've never heard the term, it means dealing with those things that are *easy pickings,* straightforward to deal with, and do not require a lot of effort. It will allow you to have many W's in the WIN column because it's easy to see why the money wasn't paid, and you (or your staff) can jump right in and zero out the balance. For example, wrong invoice numbers, incorrect addresses, and miscalculations are relatively easy fixes. Make a list of all of those that fit into this category. Create a strategy to find disconnects, which requires analysis and research. It's helpful to prioritize the list from the smallest amount to the largest and work the list. Once you get a rhythm going of solving the problems, it should motivate you to get the invoices paid.

Once you have your list, which should also include those

hard-to-crack cases, create a **tracking method,** which I like to call a **tracker**. A tracker is your aging report **plus** your *explicit, detailed* notes. It allows you to see which clients are delinquent and where they fall on the spectrum. It is a financial snapshot of where the customer falls within the collection cycles, such as their identity, contract number, items sold, etc. It allows you to see your financial picture for accounts receivables so you can get organized and decide how to move forward. Also, the more precise it is, the more useful it will be. Many tools can be used to create this system, including QuickBooks, Excel, SharePoint, and many more.

Let's review: When you start the process of collecting your funds, you will have your aging report available along with your tracker. The two work together to assist you with knowing the amount owed, which outstanding invoices will be easier to collect, the number of customers who have not paid, and which you will tackle first. Prayerfully, you will have notes in your tracker to remind you who promised to pay what and when.

Let's take it a step further. Once you have done the analysis, you should be able to parcel out the work. Remember, you don't have to take this burden on for yourself. The tracker and aging report will serve you well time and time again. They will also help others who are working with you to know *exactly* how to proceed.

Another factor that will help you be successful is to **set goals.** It's important to set goals of how much money will be collected for the week and month. For me, goals give me focus and direction for my energy and efforts. Some people use vision boards or whiteboards to see their goals. As a cash collector, I was passionate about my job and the challenges presented in collecting the cash. I knew the reward would be sweet once I met my goals.

A vision board will greet you every morning like a hot cup of coffee (or tea)! Here are some ways to make your vision board reflect your vibe:

- Find pictures that represent the feelings and possessions you want to attract into your life. Include symbols and a picture of yourself; put something humorous for those dark days so it can brighten your mood.
- Keep goals front and center.
- Print out affirmations, scriptures, favorites quotes or sayings, and positive reinforcements. Tape them around the board.
- Consider using a dry erase board. That way, you can make up-to-the minute changes as they occur.
- Use magnets, stars, highlights, or other colors to designate an action (e.g., RED might mean high priority; YELLOW might mean on pause).
- If your customers are in different time zones, visibly note the time difference to help you know when to call.
- Lastly, add anything to the board that will motivate you for the long haul.

By this point in the book, you've seen how to get ready to collect on your unpaid invoices, which has been pretty much administrative duties of creating a detailed paper trail, putting systems into place, and processes. This prep work will help you sound professional and confident when you make that phone call.

Tip #4: The Spirit of Gratitude

This last item is more than a tip. I'd like you to consider it more of a way of life. Having a spirit of gratitude is showing appreciation to your customers. Take time to send "thank you" emails to customers upon receipt of payment. Also, showing appreciation encourages future on-time payments, smoothing out the way to your company's positive cash flow. Gratitude changes everything, and... **celebrate the wins!**

Collecting a debt can be super easy or crazy difficult. That's why when you receive payment, take time to be thankful to your team, and together, celebrate a successful recovery.

I had a $23 million dollar contract to close out. The vendor and I had a discrepancy between her records and mine. My records showed that there were funds more than $500k, meaning based on the contract, it showed this amount was still available to the vendor. She sent me an email stating her records showed a payment we didn't have. I asked for proof, and she sent it as requested. I thanked her for working with me, which opened the spirit of camaraderie. That led to us doing our reconciliation, and within twenty-four hours, the contract was solved.

After the process was completed, she said, "No one calls to

say thank you." I told her it was particularly important for her to know that she helped me solve an issue. It could have been closed with an error, but instead, I worked with the client to resolve it. If I ever have to deal with this client again, I now have an ally. And that's the secret sauce! It's what makes this approach different. We are all human beings and feeling appreciated goes a long way. Relationships matter in business. The way you handle interactions will determine if you get repeat business from your customers. What you are doing is building a bridge of trust. Treat customers as insiders and tell them you understand. Collaborate to solve the problem; let them tell you what they can do. If executed correctly, you will build a long-term relationship and get the job done.

Also, try not to take yourself too seriously. Humor can diffuse an already tense and uncomfortable situation. I use humor as much as I can and keep a no-quit attitude in my back pocket.

Humor. Never leave home without it!

The Fortune is in the Follow-up

I always heard that the fortune is in the follow-up. The lack of following up results in many details being missed. It's easy to let unpaid invoices slide for a while, especially when you are busy working on other business responsibilities. However, even the smallest invoices can add up, resulting in a lot of unpaid money owed to your business. Don't be afraid to call your customer and request payment for a past due invoice. One key to my success in collecting millions of dollars was asking the necessary questions, ensuring that the client had received the invoice along with any other details needed. The follow-up is critical when collecting the cash.

In this email/text/chat world, the **telephone collection call** still reigns supreme because it is immediate, and it produces a response within moments of the connection. It is personal, allows for verbal exchange between two people, and provides the ability to obtain information in real-time. It will enable you to be flexible in your approach, changing strategy as the conversation warrants. It can result in an agreement on the next steps.

Here are some helpful tips related to the follow-up process:

- Taking notes during the collections process is much like when you visit the doctor. The doctor asks a series of questions to provide a diagnosis and the best remedy for your pain or illness. They also take notes to track the initial symptoms and treatment offered. When you return to the doctor for a follow-up, they refer to the notes to refresh their memory and document any changes. Similarly, when placing collection calls, you ask questions and take notes to diagnose why the invoice hasn't been paid, unresolved issues, and what action steps are needed to get the invoice processed for payment. In your tracker, add a column and name it "Notes". In this section, record the details of the call—who you spoke with, actions discussed, and the next steps. This is essential in the collections process. Also, follow up the call with an email to the customer so there is an email trail.
- Follow up on invoices before they are due. It will help avoid delays with payments and improve rapport with your customers. Placing a call shortly after delivery of the products or before the invoice due date is an effective

customer service tactic; it will also serve as a reminder of due payment.

- Specifically inquire if they foresee any reasons why the invoice will not be paid within terms. **Important**! Keep a record of your customer's responses.
- Customers may decide to prepay future payments along with paying the overdue invoices, so they don't miss future due dates. The bonus to this is that when you process one payment for multiple unpaid and upcoming invoices, it reduces your company's time and cost processing accounts payable. By getting paid early, you will not have to make collection calls in the future.
- Place a call to ensure all products were delivered or services were performed correctly. Ask if everything arrived on time, if there are any issues or questions, if the invoice is clear and accurate – and, of course, if the invoice has been or will soon be scheduled for payment.
- When you call, it will help to have all the specifics about the invoices you are working to collect. Having the facts in front of you will also keep you on track during the call.
- Thank the customer for their business. Build the relationship by expressing gratitude.
- Plan to follow up every week until the invoice is paid.
- Resolve any issues promptly.

Regardless of which direction the collection call goes, summarize the discussion, and outline the next steps. Reinforce payment arrangements and obtain specifics. For example, *the customer is going to make a payment in one week (note customer's name and the exact date) by check (obtain bank account information when possible), and weekly checks will continue to be sent until paid in full (confirm the dates they will be processed).* Express appreciation for the payment plan and make sure the customer writes down your address, repeating it back. Verbally review these plans and follow up via email immediately after the call to reinforce the importance of the customer keeping the agreement. After you have sent the recap email, document the conversation in your collection system, as necessary.

If payment is not received within 90 days after the due date, discuss alternative options with your manager.

Prepare for the Unexpected

What if a customer tells you that they aren't paying you or agreed to pay on a specific date but didn't make the deadline? This is an indication there is an issue that is still not resolved. Some of these issues were previously noted, such as items not received as anticipated or the customer not having the finances. There are other roadblocks you may encounter; a few are stated below.

What if your contact person is no longer employed with the company and you have to start the process over? Keeping excellent records will be vital in working with a new person, as you will probably need to recreate the situation from A–Z, and that will not be an easy task if your files are not in pristine shape. Don't be surprised if you find during your inquiry that you are at fault for why the invoice was not paid. This often happens because people do not perform quality checks, and data entry errors are made. It is important to confirm the information is entered correctly into the accounting system.

Is the company experiencing issues with any other customers? Sometimes the payment delay is due to a prime/subcontractor relationship, where one is at the other's mercy. This means the payment is dependent on multiple hands. It is important to be aware and sensitive. At the end of the day, your goal is to **collect the cash**. Due to several different circumstances and unforeseen events, you may be offered a partial payment. Unless directed otherwise, collecting half of the money is better than nothing! I recommend you take the partial payment if offered and document it in writing.

Still, with all that I've described to this point, you may experience difficulties with being paid. Here are some other ideas to recover funds, based on what type of business you own.

1. If the company is experiencing financial difficulties, you can offer to set up a payment plan. Make sure you document the agreement and ensure it is acceptable to all parties.

2. Send a strong letter demanding payment. With each request for money, make sure you include the amount owed and payment options. If you send by email, use **delivery receipt** functionality. Don't forget about the post office. Use certified mail, priority mail, or any other way to track the demand for payment.

3. For service-oriented businesses, mention discontinuing services due to lack of payment.

4. Your Accounts Payable department may add on late fees or other penalties to collect the debt.

I'm sure you've heard the phrase, "Time is money." After you have played so many rounds of tennis going back and forth while trying to collect the cash, you may have to look at your accounts and decide if taking a loss is acceptable. In that case, the amount owed by the customer would be a write-off. What you don't want is more losses than gains.

Final Thoughts and Words of Wisdom

You have been on the journey to learn how to collect the cash and win the money game. Just like an athlete gets into the zone by doing their regimen before a game, you, as a business owner, must get into the collections zone to recover your old and owed invoices. You must see yourself hitting the targets and using the various tools at your disposal to hit the bullseye.

The mindset and mental preparation are necessary to address the challenges that may come up as you recover the outstanding invoices. I wrote this book to share the strategies that have guided me to great success, and when implemented, it will do the same for you in your business. Following is an additional "**Game Day**" blueprint for success.

Pregame Collections Zone

Mental Preparation

- Focus on what you have to gain.
- Practice to build confidence; go over your script.
- Leverage your discomfort into success by giving yourself a pep talk.
- Choose your attitude; tone, pitch, and inflection are important.

Be Positive

- Have a positive outlook.
- Don't allow others to steal your joy.
- Keep an optimistic attitude.
- Refresh, release, and rejuvenate your mind when weary.

Create Momentum

- Visualize the outcome you want.
- Keep your mood upbeat; it is contagious.
- Prepare your environment; how can you be comfortable with distractions?
- Read through notes from your last successful call to get fired up and remind yourself how it felt.

Be Prepared

- Have all account information at hand.
- What is the total amount owed?
- What was purchased?
- Do you have proof of delivery?
- Was there a previous payment history?
- Were notices previously sent via email or regular mail?

Put the Odds in Your Favor

- Write down your goals.
- Clarify goals, priorities, and intentions.
- Process thoughts at a much deeper level.
- Move forward daily with focused attention.

Build Confidence

Putting it on paper…

- Motivates you to complete the task.
- Boosts your mood during and after a difficult call.
- Reminds you of previous insights that helped you address difficult calls.

Become a Problem Solver

- List obstacles you feel could prevent success.
- Mind map or storyboard/vision board to build confidence.
- Describe in detail the outcome you seek.
- Problem solvers are playful, curious, and inquisitive.

Game Time

Focused Attention

- Writing provides more clarity to the goal!
- You cannot accomplish something you cannot envision.
- Visualize the goal; ensure you have a clear understanding of the problem.

Perfect Timing

- Make calls when you have the most energy; for me, it is in the morning.
- Focus entirely on the to-do list you have developed.
- Maintain an even keel to keep you driving forward.

Time to Call

- Reaffirm your belief that today is the day!
- Roll with the punches; be ready for a little push back, but stay professional.
- Smile while you talk. It controls your style.
- Make them feel valued.

Laugh a Little/Use Humor

- This can be a tough time for the customer, so try and find something to put them at ease at the beginning of the call.
- Charisma can help you succeed.
- Kindness and humor keep the call calm and professional.

Sense the Success

- Define what success would mean to you.
- Keep track of what works.
- Be thankful and celebrate

Post-Game

Be Grateful

- Appreciation inspires a connection.
- Kindness generates a willingness to move forward to a resolution together.
- Gratitude can transform your workday and theirs!
- Make a gratitude list each week; it keeps you in a positive frame of mind. It will bring energy to your workday and help you focus.
- Note why you are grateful.

In Conclusion

- Be positive and create success in your mind.
- Push through and believe in the job you are doing.
- Do not give up; embrace even the smallest successes.
- Energy is electric; approach each call with enthusiasm.
- Build trust, which translates to long-term relationships.
- Be grateful and transform everyone's day, including yours.

Glossary of Terms

Accounts Payable (A/P): A current liability account in which a company records the amounts it owes to suppliers or vendors for goods or services received on credit.

Accounts Receivable (A/R): A current asset account in which a company records the amounts it has a right to collect from customers who received goods or services on credit.

Aging Report: An Accounts Receivable (A/R) Aging Report is a record that shows the unpaid invoice balances along with the duration for which they have been outstanding. This report helps businesses identify open invoices and allows them to keep on top of slow-paying clients. If you invoice customers for products and services and allow them to pay you some time in the future, you need to keep track of when each invoice is due, so you get paid in a timely manner.

Contracts: An agreement between a seller and a buyer. The seller agrees to deliver or sell something to a buyer for a set price that the buyer has agreed to pay. Smart business owners know that setting up a contract is essential to increasing the odds of getting paid on time. A well-structured contract covers a wide variety of variables, sets expectations, and keeps you protected in the event of a disagreement in your business relationships. While a contract in and of itself does not guarantee your invoices will be paid (the breaching of contracts does happen), it can provide you with better legal protections if your client/customer does not pay an invoice.

Customer Service: The assistance and advice provided by a company to those who buy or use its products or services.

Days Sales Outstanding (DSO): A measure of the average number of days that it takes a company to collect payment after a sale has been made.

Invoice: The primary purpose of an invoice is to provide a business and its client with a record of the sale. An invoice serves an important purpose in small business accounting; invoices demonstrate a client's obligation to pay you for your services.

Remittance: Refers to money that is sent or transferred to another party. The term is derived from the word remit, which means to send back. Remittances can be sent via a wire transfer, electronic payment system, mail, draft, or check.

Tracking System: An overall financial picture tracking tool to track how many customers you have, number of sales, invoices, how much is due, and extensive notes. The notes are really the key! System should include the following tabs:

- Customer Name
- Contract #
- Amount of Contract
- Services/Products Purchased
- Date Due to Deliver
- Invoice Submitted to Customer
- Payment Due
- Sales Rep (if applicable)
- Notes

Acknowledgements

First, I want to give honor to God for blessing me with this gift of revenue recovery. There have been several spiritual teachers along the way who sowed positive seeds within me with words of encouragement and affirmations. They have all been a blessing in my life.

I want to express my gratitude to Sharai Robbin for encouraging me to write my story and my writing coach, JC Gardner. The book *God's Creative Power for Finances* by Charles Capps opened my eyes to applying affirmations to collecting the cash. I would also like to thank all the vendors, clients, and companies that I have worked for and who have truly inspired me on this journey of collecting the cash.

Thank you to Dr. Cassandra Bradford for writing the foreword. Thanks to Sharai Robbin, Eva Jane Bunkley, Renee Myers, and Cheryl Polote-Williamson for believing in me and for their endorsements. Thanks to Dr. Cheryl Wood for giving me my first anthology opportunity that catapulted me to write this book. Thank you to Pen Legacy Publishing and Charron Monaye for accepting my book for publication.

Appendix

Appendix I:
Sample Collections Script

{Client answers}

Hello, this is [your name] with [your company name]. To whom am I speaking?

Hi, [client's name]. I'm calling to follow up on [invoice #_____] for [$ _____], which seems to be [XX] days past due. I wanted to ensure there is not a problem with the invoice and, if everything is in order, find out when payment will be made.

{Client states there is a problem}

Well, I'm sure I can get you to the right person to take care of the problem, if it's not me. What's the issue?

{Client replies with details.}

Depending on the situation, solve the issue immediately or refer them to the person who can. Document the issue so you can follow up and make sure it has been resolved and payment received. At the end, make sure you thank them! Don't forget to show gratitude.

Appendix II:
Detailed Steps for Collections

Step 1: Make the Call

- Who are you calling, and from what company are you calling?
- Which invoice are you calling about? Have handy the amount and date it was due to be paid.
- Have they (the customer) received the invoice? Note yes or no.
- If not, resend a copy via email.
- When are they scheduled to pay it?
- Record the name and title of the person you spoke with.
- Put this info in the tracker under the Notes section.

Step 2: Take Notes

- Record key points of the conversation, date, and time of the call.
- Note promises made by the customer to pay and planned payment date.
- Keep the notes organized for each client in the tracking system.
- Mark your calendar to follow up on the promise to pay.

Step 3: Leave Voicemail/Send the Email

- State who you are and the company you are calling from.
- What invoice are you calling about? Reference contract/purchase order # if applicable.
- Ask them to take a specific action to get the invoice paid.
- Leave your name, number, and email address. Say it twice slowly and follow up with an email with the same info.
- Attach a copy of the outstanding invoice.

Step 4: Ask for the Payment

- Ask why you haven't been paid (take notes).
- Show understanding; remember that collections are an extension of customer service and problem-solving.
- Remind them that they have an obligation to pay you for the product/service. Restate the amount owed and the due date. Remind them of previous promises made. Explain that you want to work with them to bring this to resolution.
- Offer a specific payment action.
- Be realistic based on information shared.
- Be in control of the conversation.
- Ask how much they can pay and when. The goal is to get the entire invoice paid in full but accept partial payments if offered.

Step 5: Just Ask for the Money

- Remember, you are a business, not a bank.
- Once you have completed all these steps, you will see that the sale is complete, and the money is in the bank.

About the Author

Dee Bowden has a Master's Degree in Management from Cambridge College and is a graduate of Steve Harvey's Act Like a Success School of Business Acceleration Program.

Dee has worked in Contract Administration and Revenue Recovery for 10+ years and has honed her skills with over a decade of experience in the corporate and public sectors.

Dee was recognized as the Face of Public Service by the Association of Government Accountants.

Dee is a Member of Alpha Kappa Alpha Sorority, Inc.

Dee is the Founder of BCS Solutions—a revenue recovery company that teaches businesses how to untangle the money disconnects, recover lost revenue, and stop leaving money on the table.

To learn more about BCS Solutions visit www.collectthecash.biz.

Dee is also a published author, contributing to two anthologies, Entrepreneurial Elevation and Soulful Prayers Vol. 2. When not recovering money, Dee enjoys listening to Smooth Jazz, Attending Wine Tastings, Concerts, Plays and riding Ferris Wheels.

Dee integrates her faith in all aspects of her personal and professional life.

CPSIA information can be obtained
at www.ICGtesting.com
Printed in the USA
LVHW072052020521
686193LV00025B/1200